PRAYER WARRIOR JOURNAL

PRAYER WARRIOR
JOURNAL

52 Weeks of Petitions, Praise, Scriptures, and Thanks to God

BARRY AND ANNELIESE ADAMS

ROCKRIDGE
PRESS

Interior and Cover Designer: Merideth Harte and Jen Cogliantry
Art Producer: Hannah Dickerson
Editor: Sean Newcott
Copyright page: Cover and interior photography, Shutterstock.
Author photo courtesy of Nick Mirka.

ISBN: Print 978-1-64611-492-4
R0

The Power of a Permanent Place for Prayers

You already know the value of recording your prayers. Whether they are listed in a notepad, written on sticky notes on your refrigerator, or stored in your mobile device, you've got them somewhere. While any record of your prayers is better than no record at all, this journal will serve as an invaluable tool to gather them all together in one place.

There is something tactile and comforting when you record a thought or prayer in your own handwriting. This journal will help organize your prayers, track the results, and prompt you to think God thoughts that are as one-of-a-kind as you are.

The more you use this prayer journal, the more precious it will be to you. For years to come, it will become a road map of your prayer journey and serve as a testimony of the Almighty's faithfulness to you and those whom you have prayed for.

WHEN YOU ARE ASKED TO PRAY

At a moment's notice, you are ready to cry out to the Almighty for any need that is presented to you. When a loved one is in trouble, your immediate response is to utter the words "Lord help _____." When there is something to celebrate, you are quick to declare, "Thank you, God!"

Your daily conversations with the Lover of your soul make it easy to commune with God, as effortlessly as you breathe. You have prayer requests somewhere, perhaps in a notebook or scribbled on scraps stuck in your Bible, or recorded on your phone.

You are probably asked to pray for others. When those around you reach the end of their rope, they turn to God for help. And when they don't feel they are connecting to God, they ask you to stand in the gap for them.

This journal is where to list all those prayer requests. It will remind you of the specific "asks" and it will also be where you track results—your answered prayers. Each recorded victory will serve as a powerful testimony of the Lord. Who knows? When you look back at your journal and remind those you have prayed for of their answered prayers, they might even be inspired to talk to the Almighty themselves!

PRAYER CHANGES THINGS

You know that prayer is important, but you might not know just how powerful your prayers are. A request made to God has the potential to transform a circumstance just because you asked. Mountains can be moved. Broken hearts can be mended. The impossible can become reality. No request is too minor and no need is too major for the Lord.

Every time you pray, you enter the courts of heaven, and the Most High attentively listens, ready to dispatch the divine host on your behalf. You are God's child, a joint heir with Jesus Christ. Your prayers matter.

The prayer of a person living right with God

is something powerful to be reckoned with.

JAMES 5:16 (MSG)

LORD, PLEASE CHANGE:

_____

_____

_____

EMBRACE YOUR
PRAYER TOOLS

Your prayer life is like a dance with the Trinity. The Holy Spirit leads you into the presence of the Creator by virtue of your union with the Redeemer, in the heavenly realms, where the impossible happens.

Your worship and intercession is a sweet-smelling sacrifice that brings much pleasure to the One who loves you with an everlasting love (Jeremiah 31:3). Your faithfulness and perseverance find beautiful expression in the many different ways you pray. Each one of your prayers is like a golden thread that weaves a beautiful tapestry in your Redeemer's presence.

With that in mind, take a moment to remind yourself of the different ways to pray and how you can enhance your prayer life in every expression of your heart to God.

MY FAVORITE PRAYER TOOLS:

_____

_____

_____

_____

_____

_____

WORSHIP AND PRAISE

Your worship is of great value in God's sight and is a powerful way to enter into the presence of your Heavenly Father with all your prayer needs. Every time you fix your eyes on the majestic beauty of the Lord, you continue to be transformed from one degree of glory to the next (2 Corinthians 3:18). Whenever you are struck with a thought of the Lord's majesty, whenever you see a glimpse of His beauty that takes your breath away, capture the moment.

WORSHIP AND PRAISE PRAYERS:

CONFESSION

You have a tender heart, so you know when issues of conscience prevent you from coming boldly into the throne room (Hebrews 4:16). Isn't it wonderful that at these times you can be assured when you confess your sins that the Source of your spirit is faithful and just to forgive you and cleanse you from all unrighteousness (1 John 1:9)? Whenever the need arises, this is the place for you to simply say "I'm sorry" to the One who loves you with an everlasting love.

PRAYERS OF CONFESSION:

_____

_____

_____

_____

_____

_____

_____

_____

_____

_____

INTERCESSION

Standing in the gap for another person is something you probably do every day whether you are aware of it or not. It is one of the most wonderful ways to enter into the high priestly ministry of Jesus (Hebrews 4:14–16) as you partner with the Holy Spirit (Romans 8:26–27). When you are carrying a friend or loved one in your heart, write their name so you can be reminded to continue to pray for them.

PRAYERS OF INTERCESSION:

THANKSGIVING

When you interlace thankfulness in every prayer, the goodness of the Most High shatters every shred of disbelief and self-pity that might try to inhibit your prayer life. Consider the many things you thank God for and gather all of them together as a testimony to Yahweh's goodness to you.

PRAYERS OF THANKS:

PETITION

You ask the Lord for help when you need it and you especially petition on behalf of others. And God loves it when you ask (Matthew 7:7–11)! Whenever a need comes to your mind, jot it down so you can then refer back to it to celebrate how many of your prayers were answered.

PRAYERS OF PETITION:

SPIRITUAL WARFARE

As a prayer warrior you know you face daily struggles with spiritual forces in the unseen realms (Ephesians 6:12). But you also know that the battle is the Lord's (2 Chronicles 20:15) so the victory has already been won in Christ. Remind yourself of heaven's perspective in every situation so you can partner with God and pray effective prayers that have divine power to demolish strongholds (2 Corinthians 10:4).

SPIRITUAL BATTLEFIELD PRAYERS:

UNION

Just as breathing is instinctive to our body, abiding in Jesus Christ can become intuitive to our spirit. Prayer is a discipline that helps us grow spiritually (John 15:5). As your inner being continues to be awakened to the nearness of the Godhead, consider the sense of union with God that comes from learning to pray without ceasing (1 Thessalonians 5:17).

PRAYERS OF UNION WITH JESUS CHRIST:

BLESSINGS

You love to bless people. It is ingrained in your spiritual DNA because you live in the waterfall of spiritual blessings in Christ (Ephesians 1:3). When you partner with God's desire to bless, you enter into a glorious level of prayer where others can experience blessings like you do.

PRAYERS OF BLESSINGS:

_____

_____

_____

_____

_____

_____

_____

_____

_____

_____

_____

_____

CONNECTING YOUR PRAYERS

A specific person or purpose often motivates you to come into the throne room with your prayer requests. Whether it is asking to comfort someone hurting or offering up thanksgiving for somebody's breakthrough, your prayers are intertwined with specific needs. Connect the dots between your prayers and everyone and everything you care about so you can be more intentional about each prayer and be mindful of its outcome.

FAMILY

Write down prayers for protection, encouragement, comfort, healing, blessing, etc., as well as daily needs for your blood relations.

PROTECTION

ENCOURAGEMENT

COMFORT

HEALING

_____

_____

_____

_____

_____

_____

_____

BLESSING

_____

_____

_____

_____

_____

_____

_____

FRIENDS

There are many ways and times you pray for those friends you care about.

PROTECTION

_____

_____

_____

_____

_____

_____

ENCOURAGEMENT

_____

_____

_____

_____

_____

_____

COMFORT

_____

_____

_____

_____

_____

HEALING

_____

_____

_____

_____

_____

BLESSING

_____

_____

_____

_____

_____

CHURCH

In addition to the ongoing needs of your church, you can pray for unity, effectiveness, growth, ministry, and a deeper appreciation for one another in your church and in other congregations.

UNITY

_____

_____

_____

_____

_____

EFFECTIVENESS

_____

_____

_____

_____

_____

GROWTH

_____

_____

_____

_____

_____

MINISTRY

_____

_____

_____

_____

_____

DEEPER APPRECIATION FOR ONE ANOTHER

_____

_____

_____

_____

_____

WORKPLACE

The people you and/or your spouse work with day in and day out
have as many needs as you do. Jot down reminders so you can
intercede on their behalf.

FAIRNESS

_____

_____

_____

_____

EMPLOYEE RELATIONS

_____

_____

_____

_____

GROWTH/PROSPERITY

_____

_____

_____

_____

PROFITABILITY

_____

_____

_____

_____

_____

INNOVATION

_____

_____

_____

_____

_____

EMPLOYEE FULFILLMENT

_____

_____

_____

_____

_____

COMMUNITY

The meaning of community to you can be as close as your neighbors or as far-flung as your city or region. Many prayers can be presented to the Lord Most High for those in your sphere of influence, including prayers for godly leaders, prosperity, and harmony.

GODLY LEADERS

PROSPERITY

HARMONY

JUSTICE

_____

_____

_____

_____

_____

SAFETY

_____

_____

_____

_____

_____

WELCOMING

_____

_____

_____

_____

_____

YOUR COUNTRY AND THE WORLD

The Bible encourages us to pray for our leaders and for all people (1 Timothy 2:1-4). When the Holy Spirit prompts you to pray about specific issues, use this guide to pray for your own country as well as other nations.

GODLY LEADERSHIP

_____

_____

_____

FOOD FOR ALL

_____

_____

_____

PROSPERITY FOR ALL

_____

_____

_____

HARMONY

_____

_____

_____

JUSTICE

_____

_____

_____

SAFETY

_____

_____

_____

FREEDOM

_____

_____

_____

FROM PULPIT/PEW TO PRAYER CLOSET

How many times have you been sitting in church and something sparked in your heart that you wanted to lift up in prayer at a later time? It might have been something your pastor said. Perhaps it was a prayer request spoken from the pulpit. Maybe it was a line in a hymn or worship song. Or you may have been in your prayer group or Bible study where needs were shared. You want to be sure to bring those to God during your quiet time talking with the Lord.

Keep this prayer journal with you at service or in meetings to jot down your thoughts; your thoughts will be there waiting for you when you are ready to take the issue to God when you enter your prayer closet.

PULPIT

_____

_____

_____

_____

_____

_____

_____

PEW (HYMN OR WORSHIP SONG)

PRAYER GROUP

GOD ANSWERS

There is absolutely no question that the Mighty One hears your prayers because of the many times and many ways your prayers have been answered over the years.

You are assured that the eyes of the Lord are upon you and heavenly ears are listening to every one of your requests (1 Peter 3:12). You also know God's response is "yes," "no," or "wait." While every outcome isn't always what you hoped for, you can rest in the promise that, in the end, all things will ultimately work together for your good (Romans 8:28).

Proverbs 19:21 (NIV) says *Many are the plans in a person's heart, but it is the Lord's purpose that prevails.* At the end of the day, you trust that the Great Shepherd's big-picture purpose will be fulfilled in your life and in the lives of those you care about. It is this foundation of trust in God's unfailing love (1 John 4:16) that carries you in every circumstance.

Sometimes the answers are immediate and sometimes there is a season of waiting. It is in these seasons of waiting that you can be strengthened by the words found in Isaiah 40:31 (NKJV): *But those who wait on the Lord shall renew their strength; They shall mount up with wings like eagles, They shall run and not be weary, They shall walk and not faint.*

You know that when God says "wait," often the Lord is looking for our perspective about a situation to change. We may think things should be worked out a certain way. (Our way!) The Most High would rather work in our hearts, allowing us to see from an eternal, heavenly perspective. This process can take time, maybe months or even years, but in the long run, our Savior's loving ways are at work in our lives and Jesus is with us every step of the way on our journey.

Whatever the result, you can rest in the fact that you can cast every concern onto your Abba's big, strong shoulders because the

Lord truly cares for you and those you care for (1 Peter 5:7). It is amazing to think that the One who has taken the time to number every hair on your head (Luke 12:7) is fully engaged with you in every aspect of life, and no detail is insignificant.

That is why it is so important to keep an ongoing record of your conversations with the Almighty. With the tyranny of the urgent, it is so easy to lose track of what you just asked for when new challenges come your way. And if you forget what you asked for, you will forget to celebrate when the answers come.

Become more intentional about recording your daily interactions with the Most High and more organized to keep track of the results. Not only will your faith be built up, but you will have the assurance that God actually answered every prayer—whether "yes," "no," or "wait". This journal will become an invaluable road map of your faith and permanent testimony of the Lord's everlasting faithfulness.

ANSWERED PRAYERS YES

ANSWERED PRAYERS NO

ANSWERED PRAYERS WAIT

FROM DEVOTION TIME
TO PRAYER TIME

In your devotional life, there is a continual illumination of your inner being. The Bible calls this revelation the Spirit of Wisdom that opens the eyes of your heart to see God (Ephesians 1:17–18).

It happens when you read a passage of Scripture for the thousandth time and yet you experience a new insight you never had before. Or maybe it occurs in your quiet time when the Holy Spirit entrusts you with a burden to pray for someone or something that seems beyond your natural scope of reason.

During these intimate devotional moments with God, many riches within your soul can be revealed. Write them down. Refer back to them and transition such moments into actionable prayers.

DEVOTIONAL REVELATIONS

_____

_____

_____

_____

_____

_____

_____

PRAYING GOD'S WORD

The Bible is the written word of God. Hebrews 4:12 says it is living and active and sharper than a double-edged sword, and has the power to divide soul and spirit. When your prayers agree with the will of the Godhead declared in the Holy Scriptures, you touch the divine power source and align yourself with God's plans and purposes.

The 50 Bible passages referenced below about prayer are refreshers to equip and empower you to continue to come boldly to the throne room. Use your favorite Bible translation to write out these much-loved Scripture passages.

1 THESSALONIANS 5:16–18

PHILIPPIANS 4:6–7

1 JOHN 5:14-15

_____

_____

_____

COLOSSIANS 4:2

_____

_____

_____

MARK 11:24

_____

_____

_____

JEREMIAH 29:12

_____

_____

_____

ROMANS 12:12

MATTHEW 6:5-8

PSALM 145:18

JEREMIAH 33:3

MATTHEW 18:20

_____

_____

_____

HEBREWS 4:16

_____

_____

_____

PSALM 18:6

_____

_____

_____

1 JOHN 5:15

_____

_____

_____

JAMES 5:16

_____

_____

_____

JAMES 1:5-6

_____

_____

_____

JOHN 15:16

_____

_____

_____

LUKE 6:27-28

_____

_____

_____

1 PETER 4:7

_____

_____

_____

JOHN 14:13

_____

_____

_____

MATTHEW 21:22

_____

_____

_____

ROMANS 8:26

_____

_____

_____

PSALM 5:3

_____

_____

_____

PSALM 118:5

_____

_____

_____

PHILIPPIANS 1:19

_____

_____

_____

PSALM 143:1

_____

_____

_____

LUKE 11:13

_____

_____

_____

PSALM 19:14

_____

_____

_____

JAMES 5:14-15

_____

_____

_____

MATTHEW 5:44

_____

_____

_____

1 PETER 3:12

_____

_____

_____

MARK 11:25

_____

_____

_____

MATTHEW 6:9–13

_____

_____

_____

PSALM 34:6

_____

_____

_____

PSALM 4:1

_____

_____

_____

ACTS 2:21

_____

_____

_____

1 CHRONICLES 16:11

_____

_____

_____

2 CHRONICLES 7:14

_____

_____

_____

EPHESIANS 6:18

_____

_____

_____

JAMES 5:13

_____

_____

_____

PROVERBS 15:8

_____

_____

_____

PSALM 17:6

_____

_____

_____

PSALM 102:17

_____

_____

_____

PSALM 141:2

_____

_____

_____

PROVERBS 15:29

_____

_____

_____

MATTHEW 7:7–11

_____

_____

_____

LUKE 18:1

_____

_____

_____

1 TIMOTHY 2:8

_____

_____

_____

1 JOHN 1:9

_____

_____

_____

1 TIMOTHY 2:1-2

_____

_____

_____

GOD'S PROMISES

The Bible says God keeps His promises. It is important for us to believe that, because when we do, we demonstrate our trust in God.

Proverbs 3:5-6 says *Trust God from the bottom of your heart; don't try to figure out everything on your own. Listen for God's voice in everything you do, everywhere you go; he's the one who will keep you on track* (MSG).

Over the years, you know this to be true. Your life is proof that God is the ultimate promise keeper and is trustworthy time and time again. Think about how many times you have trusted the Lord with details and circumstances beyond your control and how the living God came through for you and those you care about.

In this section, take the opportunity to say "yes" and "amen" (2 Corinthians 1:20) to 20 precious Bible promises that have been declared over you from heaven. Look up these much-loved passages and write them down using the Bible translation of your choice. Then pray about how God has kept these promises.

JOSHUA 23:14

ROMANS 4:20-21

_____

_____

_____

PSALM 37:4

_____

_____

_____

MARK 11:24

_____

_____

_____

PHILIPPIANS 4:19

_____

_____

_____

2 CORINTHIANS 1:20

_____

_____

_____

ISAIAH 40:31

_____

_____

_____

ISAIAH 41:10

_____

_____

_____

ISAIAH 43:2

_____

_____

_____

ISAIAH 40:29

_____

_____

_____

JEREMIAH 29:11

_____

_____

_____

JOHN 8:36

_____

_____

_____

JOSHUA 1:9

_____

_____

_____

ROMANS 8:28

_____

_____

_____

PHILIPPIANS 4:6-7

_____

_____

_____

PROVERBS 3:5-6

_____

_____

_____

MATTHEW 6:31-33

_____

_____

_____

LUKE 11:9–13

_____

_____

_____

JOHN 14:13–16

_____

_____

_____

PSALM 86:5

_____

_____

_____

PSALM 34:17

_____

_____

_____

DEUTERONOMY 31:8

_____

_____

_____

EXODUS 14:14

_____

_____

_____

JAMES 4:7

_____

_____

_____

JAMES 1:5

_____

_____

_____

ISAIAH 54:17

_____

_____

_____

JOHN 11:25-26

_____

_____

_____

JAMES 1:12

_____

_____

_____

JOHN 14:2-3

_____

_____

_____

BEYOND WORDS

A much-quoted statement attributed to an Italian Catholic friar in the thirteenth century, St. Francis of Assisi, says *Preach the Gospel at all times. When necessary, use words.* Prayer can often be like that. Much of an active prayer life is nonverbal and seemingly intangible. Such is the realm of the Spirit. 2 Corinthians 4:18 (NIV) reminds us to *fix our eyes not on what is seen, but on what is unseen, since what is seen is temporary, but what is unseen is eternal.* So it should be no surprise when your prayer life goes way beyond your conscious understanding.

Have there been times in your prayer life that words fail to describe? What about those indescribable moments when all you were left with was a sigh, or a picture in your mind's eye, or an impression? Perhaps a dream you had in the middle of the night needs to be journaled. Or maybe an ethereal feeling connected to an emotion due to pain, grief or loss.

This section is devoted to these sacred times in your prayer life where words are simply not enough. This is the place to capture your God thoughts, your divine appointments, and all the holy interactions that are stirred deep within you by the Lover of your soul that can sometimes defy logic and reason.

On these pages, you can ask God to help you bring form to the formless, understanding to the mysteries, and substance to the eternal realities. Record what goes way beyond words, where heaven meets earth in the holy realm of your heart. And know it is both real and sacred.

52 WEEKS OF PRAYER

WEEK 1 | *Date:* _____

WHAT I'M THANKFUL FOR . . .

○ *An answered prayer*   ○ *Family and friends*

○ *A personal breakthrough*   ○ *Other:* _____

A KEY VERSE:

_____

_____

_____

_____

_____

_____

_____

_____

_____

_____

My Prayers this week:

WEEK 2 | *Date:* _____

WHAT GOD IS TEACHING ME . . .

○ *I am loved*   ○ *I am His child*

○ *I am forgiven*   ○ *Other:* _____

MY KEY VERSE:

_____

_____

_____

_____

_____

_____

_____

_____

_____

My Prayers this week:

WEEK 3 | *Date:*_____

ATTRIBUTES OF GOD THAT I'M THINKING ABOUT . . .

○ *God's love*   ○ *God's compassion*

○ *God's mercy*   ○ *God's patience*

○ *God's faithfulness*   ○ *Other:*_____

○ *God's power*

A KEY SCRIPTURE:

_____

_____

_____

_____

_____

_____

_____

_____

My Prayers this week:

WEEK 4 | *Date:* _____

A REMINDER TO PRAY FOR . . .

○ *Family or friends* ○ *My community/country*

○ *Coworkers* ○ *Other:* _____

○ *My church*

A SCRIPTURE I'M CLAIMING:

_____

_____

_____

_____

_____

_____

_____

_____

_____

My Prayers this week:

WEEK 5 | *Date:* _____

HOW GOD HAS REVEALED HIMSELF . . .

O *Friend*

O *Savior*

O *Protector*

O *Comforter*

O *Provider*

O *Father*

O *Other:* _____

A PROMISE:

_____

_____

_____

_____

_____

_____

_____

_____

My Prayers this week:

WEEK 6 | *Date:* _____

THIS WEEK'S FOCUS ON FRUITFULNESS . . .

- ○ *Love*
- ○ *Joy*
- ○ *Peace*
- ○ *Patience*
- ○ *Kindness*

- ○ *Goodness*
- ○ *Faithfulness*
- ○ *Gentleness*
- ○ *Self-control*

GALATIANS 5:22–23:

_____

_____

_____

_____

_____

_____

_____

My Prayers this week:

WEEK 7 | *Date:* _____

SOMETHING TO CELEBRATE . . .

○ *A personal breakthrough*   ○ *An unexpected blessing*

○ *An answered prayer*   ○ *Other:* _____

○ *A salvation*

MY KEY VERSE:

_____

_____

_____

_____

_____

_____

_____

_____

My Prayers this week:

WEEK 8 | *Date:* _____

WHAT GOD LOVES ABOUT ME . . .

○ *My quirkiness*

○ *My smile*

○ *My personality*

○ *My passion*

○ *My perseverance*

○ *My faithfulness*

○ *My unique talents*

○ *My enthusiasm*

○ *My intellect*

○ *Other:* _____

THIS WEEK'S SCRIPTURE:

_____

_____

_____

_____

_____

_____

_____

My Prayers this week:

WEEK 9 | *Date:* _____

WHAT I AM BELIEVING FOR THIS WEEK . . .

○ *Me*

○ *Others*

○ *Restoration*

○ *Healing*

○ *Reconciliation*

○ *Encouragement*

○ *Salvation*

○ *Provision*

○ *Other:* _____

THIS WEEK'S BIBLE PASSAGE:

_____

_____

_____

_____

_____

_____

_____

My Prayers this week:

WEEK 10 | *Date:* _____

A REMINDER TO PRAY FOR . . .

○ *My spiritual growth*   ○ *Church*

○ *Family*   ○ *Community*

○ *Friends*   ○ *Country*

○ *Coworkers*   ○ *Other:* _____

THIS WEEK'S WORD:

_____

_____

_____

_____

_____

_____

_____

My Prayers this week:

WEEK 11 | *Date:* _____

I'M IN AWE OF GOD'S . . .

- ○ *Majesty*
- ○ *Love*
- ○ *Compassion*
- ○ *Omnipotence*
- ○ *Omniscience*

- ○ *Omnipresence*
- ○ *Faithfulness*
- ○ *Kindness*
- ○ *Gentleness*
- ○ *Other:* _____

A LINKED SCRIPTURE:

_____

_____

_____

_____

_____

_____

_____

My Prayers this week:

WEEK 12 | *Date:* _____

WAYS GOD IS TEACHING ME THIS WEEK . . .

- ○ *Church sermon*
- ○ *Bible study*
- ○ *Personal devotions*
- ○ *From an experience*

- ○ *By a friend*
- ○ *Through work*
- ○ *Other:* _____

A SCRIPTURE THAT STANDS OUT:

_____

_____

_____

_____

_____

_____

_____

_____

My Prayers this week:

WEEK 13 | *Date:* _____

I'M LEARNING TO TRUST GOD WHEN . . .

_____

_____

_____

LINKED SCRIPTURE:

_____

_____

_____

_____

_____

_____

_____

_____

_____

_____

My Prayers this week:

WEEK 14 | *Date:* _____

LORD, HELP ME LEAN ON YOU IN
THIS AREA OF MY LIFE . . .

_____

_____

_____

KEY VERSE:

_____

_____

_____

_____

_____

_____

_____

_____

_____

_____

My Prayers this week:

WEEK 15 | *Date:* _____

IN MY LIFE, FATHER HAS SHOWN ME HE IS TRUSTWORTHY IN THESE AREAS . . .

_____

_____

_____

AN IMPORTANT BIBLE PASSAGE:

_____

_____

_____

_____

_____

_____

_____

_____

_____

_____

_____

My Prayers this week:

WEEK 16 | *Date:* _____

SOMEONE WHO I'M PRAYING FOR THIS WEEK:

_____

SOMEONE WHO IS PRAYING FOR ME THIS WEEK:

_____

A PROMISE I'M CLAIMING:

_____

_____

_____

_____

_____

_____

_____

_____

_____

My Prayers this week:

WEEK 17 | *Date:* _____

WHAT I'M THANKFUL FOR . . .

○ *An answered prayer*   ○ *Family and friends*

○ *A personal breakthrough*   ○ *Other:* _____

A KEY VERSE:

_____

_____

_____

_____

_____

_____

_____

_____

_____

My Prayers this week:

WEEK 18 | *Date:* _____

WHAT GOD IS TEACHING ME THIS WEEK . . .

○ *I am loved*   ○ *I am His child*

○ *I am forgiven*   ○ *Other:* _____

MY KEY VERSE:

_____

_____

_____

_____

_____

_____

_____

_____

_____

_____

_____

_____

My Prayers this week:

WEEK 19 | *Date:* _____

ATTRIBUTES OF GOD THAT I'M THINKING ABOUT . . .

○ *God's love*

○ *God's mercy*

○ *God's faithfulness*

○ *God's power*

○ *God's compassion*

○ *God's patience*

○ *Other:* _____

A KEY SCRIPTURE:

_____

_____

_____

_____

_____

_____

_____

_____

My Prayers this week:

WEEK 20 | *Date:* _____

A REMINDER TO PRAY FOR . . .

○ *Family or friends*   ○ *My community/country*

○ *Coworkers*   ○ *Other:* _____

○ *My church*

A SCRIPTURE I'M CLAIMING:

_____

_____

_____

_____

_____

_____

_____

_____

My Prayers this week:

WEEK 21 | *Date:* _____

_____

HOW GOD HAS REVEALED HIMSELF THIS WEEK . . .

○ *Friend*

○ *Provider*

○ *Savior*

○ *Father*

○ *Protector*

○ *Other:* _____

○ *Comforter*

THIS WEEK'S PROMISE:

_____

_____

_____

_____

_____

_____

_____

_____

_____

My Prayers this week:

WEEK 22 | *Date:* _____

THIS WEEK'S FOCUS ON FRUITFULNESS . . .

○ *Love*

○ *Joy*

○ *Peace*

○ *Patience*

○ *Kindness*

○ *Goodness*

○ *Faithfulness*

○ *Gentleness*

○ *Self-control*

GALATIANS 5:22–23:

_____

_____

_____

_____

_____

_____

_____

My Prayers this week:

WEEK 23 | *Date:* _____

SOMETHING TO CELEBRATE . . .

○ *A personal breakthrough*   ○ *An unexpected blessing*

○ *An answered prayer*   ○ *Other:* _____

○ *A salvation*

MY KEY VERSE:

_____

_____

_____

_____

_____

_____

_____

_____

_____

_____

My Prayers this week:

WEEK 24 | *Date:* _____

WHAT GOD LOVES ABOUT ME . . .

○ *My quirkiness*

○ *My smile*

○ *My personality*

○ *My passion*

○ *My perseverance*

○ *My faithfulness*

○ *My unique talents*

○ *My enthusiasm*

○ *My intellect*

○ *Other:* _____

THIS WEEK'S SCRIPTURE:

_____

_____

_____

_____

_____

_____

My Prayers this week:

WEEK 25 | *Date:* _____

WHAT I AM BELIEVING FOR THIS WEEK . . .

○ *Me*

○ *Others*

○ *Restoration*

○ *Healing*

○ *Reconciliation*

○ *Encouragement*

○ *Salvation*

○ *Provision*

○ *Other:* _____

THIS WEEK'S BIBLE PASSAGE:

_____

_____

_____

_____

_____

_____

My Prayers this week:

WEEK 26 | *Date:* _____

A REMINDER TO PRAY FOR . . .

- ○ *My spiritual growth*
- ○ *Family*
- ○ *Friends*
- ○ *Coworkers*

- ○ *Church*
- ○ *Community*
- ○ *Country*
- ○ *Other:* _____

THIS WEEK'S WORD:

_____

_____

_____

_____

_____

_____

_____

_____

My Prayers this week:

WEEK 27 | *Date:*_____

I'M IN AWE OF GOD'S . . .

- ○ *Majesty*
- ○ *Love*
- ○ *Compassion*
- ○ Omnipotence
- ○ Omniscience

- ○ *Omnipresence*
- ○ *Faithfulness*
- ○ *Kindness*
- ○ *Gentleness*
- ○ *Other:*_____

A LINKED SCRIPTURE:

_____

_____

_____

_____

_____

_____

_____

My Prayers this week:

WEEK 28 | *Date:* _____

WAYS GOD IS TEACHING ME THIS WEEK . . .

○ *Church sermon*   ○ *By a friend*

○ *Bible study*   ○ *Through work*

○ *Personal devotions*   ○ *Other:* _____

○ *From an experience*

A SCRIPTURE THAT STANDS OUT:

_____

_____

_____

_____

_____

_____

_____

_____

My Prayers this week:

I'M LEARNING TO TRUST GOD WHEN . . .

_____

_____

_____

LINKED SCRIPTURE:

_____

_____

_____

_____

_____

_____

_____

_____

_____

_____

_____

My Prayers this week:

WEEK 30 | *Date:* _____

LORD, HELP ME LEAN ON YOU IN
THIS AREA OF MY LIFE . . .

_____

_____

_____

KEY VERSE:

_____

_____

_____

_____

_____

_____

_____

_____

_____

_____

_____

My Prayers this week:

WEEK 31 | *Date:* _____

IN MY LIFE, FATHER HAS SHOWN ME HE IS TRUSTWORTHY IN THESE AREAS . . .

_____

_____

_____

AN IMPORTANT BIBLE PASSAGE:

_____

_____

_____

_____

_____

_____

_____

_____

_____

_____

My Prayers this week:

WEEK 32 | *Date:* _____

SOMEONE WHO I'M PRAYING FOR THIS WEEK:

_____

SOMEONE WHO IS PRAYING FOR ME THIS WEEK:

_____

A PROMISE I'M CLAIMING:

_____

_____

_____

_____

_____

_____

_____

_____

_____

_____

My Prayers this week:

WEEK 33 | *Date:* _____

WHAT I'M THANKFUL FOR THIS WEEK . . .

○ *An answered prayer*   ○ *Family and friends*

○ *A personal breakthrough*   ○ *Other:* _____

A KEY VERSE:

_____

_____

_____

_____

_____

_____

_____

_____

_____

_____

My Prayers this week:

WEEK 34 | *Date:*_____

WHAT GOD IS TEACHING ME THIS WEEK . . .

○ *I am loved*   ○ *I am His child*

○ *I am forgiven*   ○ *Other:*_____

MY KEY VERSE:

_____

_____

_____

_____

_____

_____

_____

_____

_____

_____

_____

My Prayers this week:

WEEK 35 | *Date:* _____

ATTRIBUTES OF GOD THAT I'M THINKING ABOUT THIS WEEK . . .

- ○ *God's love*
- ○ *God's mercy*
- ○ *God's faithfulness*
- ○ *God's power*

- ○ *God's compassion*
- ○ *God's patience*
- ○ *Other:* _____

A KEY SCRIPTURE:

_____

_____

_____

_____

_____

_____

_____

_____

My Prayers this week:

WEEK 36 | *Date:* _____

A REMINDER TO PRAY FOR . . .

○ *Family or friends*　　　○ *My community/country*

○ *Coworkers*　　　　　　○ *Other:* _____

○ *My church*

A SCRIPTURE I'M CLAIMING:

_____

_____

_____

_____

_____

_____

_____

_____

_____

_____

My Prayers this week:

WEEK 37 | *Date:* _____

HOW GOD HAS REVEALED HIMSELF THIS WEEK . . .

○ *Friend*   ○ *Provider*

○ *Savior*   ○ *Father*

○ *Protector*   ○ *Other:* _____

○ *Comforter*

THIS WEEK'S PROMISE:

_____

_____

_____

_____

_____

_____

_____

_____

My Prayers this week:

WEEK 38 | *Date:* _____

THIS WEEK'S FOCUS ON FRUITFULNESS . . .

○ *Love*

○ *Joy*

○ *Peace*

○ *Patience*

○ *Kindness*

○ *Goodness*

○ *Faithfulness*

○ *Gentleness*

○ *Self-control*

GALATIANS 5:22–23:

_____

_____

_____

_____

_____

_____

_____

My Prayers this week:

WEEK 39 | *Date:* _____

SOMETHING TO CELEBRATE...

○ *A personal breakthrough*   ○ *An unexpected blessing*

○ *An answered prayer*   ○ *Other:* _____

○ *A salvation*

MY KEY VERSE:

_____

_____

_____

_____

_____

_____

_____

_____

_____

_____

My Prayers this week:

WEEK 40 | *Date:* _____

WHAT GOD LOVES ABOUT ME . . .

- ○ *My quirkiness*
- ○ *My smile*
- ○ *My personality*
- ○ *My passion*
- ○ *My perseverance*

- ○ *My faithfulness*
- ○ *My unique talents*
- ○ *My enthusiasm*
- ○ *My intellect*
- ○ *Other:* _____

THIS WEEK'S SCRIPTURE:

_____

_____

_____

_____

_____

_____

_____

_____

My Prayers this week:

WEEK 41 | *Date:* _____

WHAT I AM BELIEVING FOR THIS WEEK . . .

- ○ *Me*
- ○ *Others*
- ○ *Restoration*
- ○ *Healing*
- ○ *Reconciliation*

- ○ *Encouragement*
- ○ *Salvation*
- ○ *Provision*
- ○ *Other:* _____

A KEY BIBLE PASSAGE:

_____

_____

_____

_____

_____

_____

_____

My Prayers this week:

WEEK 42 | *Date:* _____

A REMINDER TO PRAY THIS WEEK FOR . . .

○ *My spiritual growth*   ○ *Church*

○ *Family*   ○ *Community*

○ *Friends*   ○ *Country*

○ *Coworkers*   ○ *Other:* _____

THIS WEEK'S WORD:

_____

_____

_____

_____

_____

_____

_____

_____

My Prayers this week:

WEEK 43 | *Date:* _____

I'M IN AWE OF GOD'S . . .

- ○ *Majesty*
- ○ *Love*
- ○ *Compassion*
- ○ *Omnipotence*
- ○ *Omniscience*

- ○ *Omnipresence*
- ○ *Faithfulness*
- ○ *Kindness*
- ○ *Gentleness*
- ○ *Other:* _____

A LINKED SCRIPTURE:

_____

_____

_____

_____

_____

_____

_____

My Prayers this week:

WEEK 44 | *Date:* _____

WAYS GOD IS TEACHING ME THIS WEEK . . .

○ *Church sermon*

○ *Bible study*

○ *Personal devotions*

○ *From an experience*

○ *By a friend*

○ *Through work*

○ *Other:* _____

A SCRIPTURE THAT STANDS OUT:

_____

_____

_____

_____

_____

_____

_____

My Prayers this week:

WEEK 45 | *Date:* _____

I'M LEARNING TO TRUST GOD WHEN . . .

_____

_____

_____

LINKED SCRIPTURE:

_____

_____

_____

_____

_____

_____

_____

_____

_____

_____

_____

My Prayers this week:

WEEK 46 | *Date:* _____

LORD, HELP ME LEAN ON YOU IN
THIS AREA OF MY LIFE . . .

_____

_____

_____

KEY VERSE:

_____

_____

_____

_____

_____

_____

_____

_____

_____

_____

My Prayers this week:

WEEK 47 | *Date:* _____

IN MY LIFE, FATHER HAS SHOWN ME HE IS TRUSTWORTHY IN THESE AREAS . . .

_____

_____

_____

AN IMPORTANT BIBLE PASSAGE:

_____

_____

_____

_____

_____

_____

_____

_____

_____

My Prayers this week:

WEEK 48 | *Date:* _____

SOMEONE WHO I'M PRAYING FOR THIS WEEK:

_____

SOMEONE WHO IS PRAYING FOR ME THIS WEEK:

_____

A PROMISE I'M CLAIMING:

_____
_____
_____
_____
_____
_____
_____
_____
_____

My Prayers this week:

WEEK 49 | *Date:* _____

WHAT I'M THANKFUL FOR THIS WEEK . . .

○ *An answered prayer*   ○ *Family and friends*

○ *A personal breakthrough*   ○ *Other:* _____

A KEY VERSE:

_____

_____

_____

_____

_____

_____

_____

_____

_____

_____

My Prayers this week:

WEEK 50 | *Date:* _____

WHAT GOD IS TEACHING ME THIS WEEK . . .

○ *I am loved*   ○ *I am His child*

○ *I am forgiven*   ○ *Other:* _____

MY KEY VERSE:

_____

_____

_____

_____

_____

_____

_____

_____

_____

My Prayers this week:

WEEK 51 | *Date:* _____

ATTRIBUTES OF GOD THAT I'M THINKING ABOUT THIS WEEK . . .

○ *God's love*   ○ *God's compassion*

○ *God's mercy*   ○ *God's patience*

○ *God's faithfulness*   ○ *Other:* _____

○ *God's power*

A KEY SCRIPTURE:

_____

_____

_____

_____

_____

_____

_____

_____

My Prayers this week:

WEEK 52 | *Date:* _____

A REMINDER TO PRAY FOR...

○ *Family or friends*   ○ *My community/country*

○ *Coworkers*   ○ *Other:* _____

○ *My church*

A SCRIPTURE I'M CLAIMING:

_____

_____

_____

_____

_____

_____

_____

_____

_____

_____

My Prayers this week:

About the Authors

Barry and his wife, Anneliese, have been married for more than 37 years and have three grown children and three spectacular grandchildren. After spending 19 years in the newspaper advertising business, Barry entered pastoral ministry, where a sermon illustration he created called "Father's Love Letter" went viral on the internet starting in 1999.

In early 2000, Barry and Anneliese founded Father Heart Communications to help them facilitate the growing demand for their new international ministry to share God's love around the world. Since that time, they have traveled together, and their adventures have taken them to five continents.

Their three main websites are FathersLoveLetter.com, 365Promises.com, and Fatherheart.tv.

They live in Jordan Station, Ontario, Canada.